# Breaking the Darkness

A journey through pain and healing
from Depression

Srivalli Gottumukkala

BookLeaf
Publishing

India | USA | UK

Presentation by *BookLeaf Publishing*

Web: www.bookleafpub.com

E-mail: info@bookleafpub.com


ISBN: 9789358310108

First edition 2023

# DEDICATION

This one's for me...for trying to come back
around to myself.

# PREFACE

Give yourself grace, living is hard, loving is
harder.

# Fairytale

I do not know where to put you, where you live
inside me, absence makes you forgetful, makes
me build up red for you, it pulses and warms and
warns, it is the sun when you are gone and I
think how lovely, I think how wide, I think how
silent night is, and easy the TV shows I choose,
how anxious I am the phone might ring.

I hate that sound.

But you wouldn't know because you say sweet
things and I count words more important than
truth, not all words, just the ones comfortable in
imaginary places, the ones I'd pocket for weight
falling from anyone's mouth, the ones I want to
mean when I say them to you but I think they
have already been wrung dry, for that weight just
over my shoulders, for his smell and large hand
with a bent thumb fitting that small hollow in
my lower back, so now I hold your words,
before I offer them to you, I check but already
know they're hollow.

So even the things that are your fault can't be
cause I haven't said no, not in the way that

means stop. I have said maybe and possibly or yes. That is the worst of them. That yes. That sometimes when I'm looking at you seems perfect, seems better than the sun that comes when you're gone – but it holds for just the seconds before you're made you and I wish I'd said less that first day, wish I hadn't wanted enough to forgot that a person comes with meeting need, wish I'd known enough to close my eyes and see that alone fit nice too.

How much of that is love, and how much is that you ain't love for me? I say you are and I'm sorry for that, you'll hate me and somehow even that seems better than keeping you.

I don't know if love is born eager only once, if it is young and sly and says I will be your everything if this is where you want me to fit, in this man's shape, in this outline of future, but choose wisely because there is only space for recklessness once; any coming after will be watered down knowing with the sound of cracks between people, with how much easier it is to balance instead of fall.

I say maybe because that's what people say but I know it ain't you. You were not who you said you were, you were confusion and you were obligation, the downside of my tenacity for loyalty and it was still not you. It was me. It is me. I am learning love, I am remembering it, and it is ruining me.

3

# Take The Last of Me, Too

I wish that first day I'd just
waved hello
from a distance or maybe relented
enough for that first kiss; cause they were good
kisses. So maybe
kisses and then
nothing
then just what could've been your face and the
sound of your laugh set to romantic comedy
soundtracks harmless and
soft around the edges. But then where
would be my more?
In the end I desire cause of you … in spite of
you?
some mornings it's difficult knowing which, it's
only steady
in staying
tied
to you.
When we're old we'll have this conversation
when we're old and she's no longer concerned
when teeth
can be pulled free and body
once eager finds energy best spent in
sagging

to

the

floor

we will say and chuckle 'round them things
belonging to us alone we'll hold hands choosing
validation over love we'll kiss
with them kisses done when there's nothing left
to do we'll

remember

it as a love

story

as words on paper as chapters that can
close we'll walk back to the end of life, back to
storing our sepiaed pages on dusty shelves
i'll say to myself, lay you down
i'll say thank you and mean it every single time

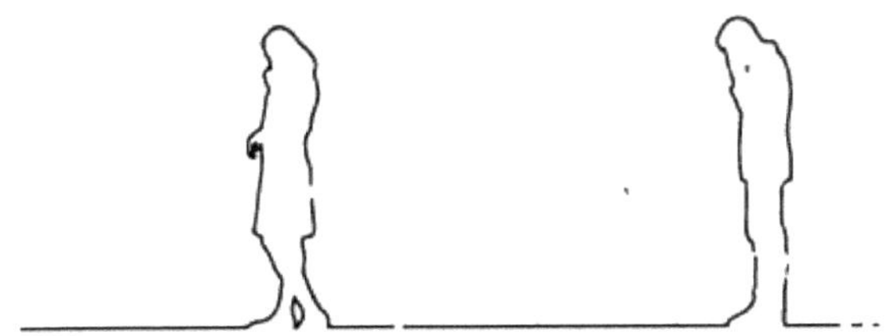

# 4 Bourbons In

how many people can I loan myself to
not sure but looking out I think the next one
could be you
see no matter how hard I try I am tempted by the
feeling of a man's hands on my thighs, kisses
that can seem real, that clothes shedding sex
appeal found in the curve of neck or that naked
show of skin from wrist to edge of pushed up
sleeve, I know you're teasing me, want to see
what I'm working with, want to convince me
that laying down is worth jumping around
excitement in not having forever, in having to
push it all to fit in just one night, and right now
that shit really does sound right, plus you found
that spot I never talk about, I feel the warmth of
your breath there and your hands are pulling on
my hair so how wrong could it be, me wanting
you, you wanting me, we could make the perfect
song and you could play the chorus all night
long, but I'm looking for the bridge, looking for
that part that lives past the light of sunrise or
having to look in someone's eyes
how many people can I loan myself to
not sure but looking out I think the next one
could be you

see it seems an ample sacrifice, to thinking twice
or walking away, the fact that I tried I think
means you should stay, your tongue on my
breast locks away tears, glue to a heart just
fractured instead, until you shift your weight
from my bed, then too much room to think, to
wonder to dream, it's heavy my skin too slick to
carry such a thing but holding you I can do so
i'll call again, think if I can't reach you then I
might just take your friend, shake it off as just
one time, only really need to feel guilty if you
were mine. But we've worked it out an
arrangement between friends, think even if you
knew you'd still call me again, plus soon I'll be
done, no more priceless exchange, I'll hold out
for the man who means it when he says my
name. But not tonight, tonight you'll come
through and even if you don't I'm sure I'll make
due
how many people can I loan myself to
not sure but looking out I think the next one
could be you.

# Epiphany

There's an impression in the carpet left by the weight of your boot. I watch the awakened fibers rise and imagine you ambivalent in unceasing sunshine singing along with the radio adjusting the forgotten with words you create, the window's down and when the air brings scent of me, lavender from the garden you pass that hints my perfume, honey sweet donuts at a roadside stand reminiscent of the night when sticky sweetness hid in crevices rolled over mounds of brownness before blessed by warm tongues and impatient lips you cough maybe, rub the spot rubbed bare by years of forgotten habit behind the curve of your left ear roll the window tight and decide it won't use too much gas to run the air, even though now coolness from the open vents seems intrusive, excessive, warmth becomes like the moral at the end of forgotten fables. Somewhere in the midst of thinking, yours now that mine still clings to an imprint hesitating as if it knows it is the last you'll ever leave, return becomes a possibility, walking through a door that seemed ever revolving, finding peace in comfort turned to silence, numbing resistance bearable and known, maybe

pushing underneath love that's been rolled and
bruised until it's forgotten its shape, place and is
content to sit at partially lit tables and read the
same Sunday paper in silence but before you
decide, the imprint tempts movement, all that
was of you is gone and though the sun has long
past set, in new darkness I see the meaning of
me for the first time since our time isn't my time
and realize my shape is slender without your
weight.

# A Caregiver's Prayer

Here's the thing, I didn't ask for any of this, but
it doesn't matter. The older I get I'm clear life is
meant for living me, for wearing my skin
patchworked dangling my name, my family, my
heritage, my wishes, prayers and wants I'm too
scared to whisper climbing some Everest to
happy
but life don't care if I am
life only cares that I keep to living, and it'll ride
my skin till the wheels fall off
and then what?
then if I'm lucky there's enough people left
behind willing to bury me in the ground or
spread my ashes someplace where the air feels
clean
when I was younger I was going to be a writer, I
started novels handwritten in three ring binders
and read books til my eyes burned and my
shoulders ached from propping myself in
exchange for one more chapter
when I was younger, I was going to be in love.
it wasn't a fairytale.
It wasn't that kind of childhood, but it felt safe,
even with its undefined edges, it was enough of
a thing to keep me looking forward. I was going

to be a writer in love, not in New York or Los
Angeles, where everyday would end feeling
same as left undone
i was going to find land filled with trees, giant
ones growing tall enough for blocking the sky,
so the nights'd be black enough for disappearing
rest
til the sun pushed light enough through them
trees there was no denying it was time for
another day, and it'd be okay, cause the night
would be waiting.
It was all supposed to be so simple. It was such a
small dream, pocket-sized. But nobody's
deserving of a dream, no matter how tiny it is.
You can work for it, and hard work's a stepping
stone, hard work is hope til it ain't
cause in the end still life decides
in the end life is wearing me like a skin till the
wheels fall off
i ended up a caregiver.
There should be better words for an accident
than an accident, or the unexpected, or tragedy
pulling past my heart, to them strings thick with
blood keeping me off balance when I walk or
sleep or breathe or be reminded the life of the
person I love most needs mine to keep to ticking
my own life wearing me like a skin, all while
hers is resting like an hourglass with a leak in
the palm of my hands, and I can't never get 'em

clean enough for not feeling the grit. It lingers
and I hate, same way I'm thankful, it makes me
check that she's breathing at three in the
morning
it's why we made it to the hospital in time,
doctors saying I was doing a good job taking
care
of her
then meeting my eyes for pulling me away from
her bed with all those tubes and machines
ticking like a bomb to discuss leaving the
hospital alone
since then I been working hard at giving life a
run for her money, cause there's a numbness
inside turning dangerous, makes me walk
through days like I can't feel hard under my feet
or the breeze when it blows, like it just passes
me
bye, cause it ain't enough me
left
there
or cause the me I am ain't worth it. My mom
will be okay
i've got new doctor's appointments in my phone,
backed up in a thin planner and written in
smudge-proof ink
i've budgeted for new meds, bought sleeping
wedges to keep her back elevated, EKG and
blood pressure machines, moved work hours

around to build a surplus of time in the day, I
meal prep on Sundays, Saturdays are for
cleaning, I buy her stuffed animals, sloths and
monkeys, one so soft it feels fake with a heating
pad tummy activated by ninety seconds in the
microwave
it's for laying over her stomach when the pain
stands up asking for it, but mostly she holds it
like the grandbaby I'll never give her
i sleep in a room feeling same as a burning haze
yellow mostly thin and leaking from every night
light plugged into every outlet in case she gets
up at night, but it don't matter, I always hear her,
and even when I don't I'm up to check with my
arms already reaching to steady her stride,
firming my middle so she can use me for
balance
she looks at me and says thank you and them
strings fighting to pull me off my square can't
reach past my love for her, even as it feels like
it's the life living me going through it, while the
real me, the one remembering writing and
waiting for night next to trees, and falling in
love free of fairytale, well, she's mostly busy
just trying to keep breathing.
saying
i never asked for it
sounds selfish cause my mom ain't ask either.
she was healthy and strong, singing good

morning and doing yoga in the sunshine so the
brown of her skin carried a halo like it was
blessed.
Maybe that's why we ain't see it coming, but I
figure the real truth is nobody does.
She was a glowing aura of blessing till I made a
surprise weekend visit and her beautiful brown
was gray, she looked at me with eyes working to
stay afloat and doubled over from the energy it
took to brush her teeth. And then
we never discussed it.
For what?
she was my momma, she was sick and my
stepdad locked away with a recliner and Sunday
newspapers, cigars and an NFL streaming
package and then talked to coworkers about
in sickness and in health
but he never came to the hospital, not after eight
surgeries and doctors looking at me and momma
saying she was an anomaly, we'd treat
symptoms until the core could be pulled loose
and nobody came to the hospital
this last time
when she almost died
when my eyes stayed stuck to those monitors for
every sign the doctors warned me about, praying
at every dip to rise right back up same as Jesus
raising Lazarus from the grave. I ain't sleep for
two days sitting by that hospital bed, all while

momma forgot who I was, got close enough to
death she saw people coming through the walls
and angels floating by her bed waiting for her to
decide. Nobody
showed up then not my
stepdaddy
not my sister
or my aunt and that there is the end
of my family, so tiny it should've been an easy
decision, so tiny us being together should have
been a given, but nobody deserves anything, and
hope is a heavy lie sometimes, too.
That was two weeks ago, and part of me's steady
reconciling the difference cause since the
weekend of my brown momma turning gray it's
been eleven years. Eleven years weaving into
what she'd need till that was the bulk of the skin
my life was wearing, and it was stretched tight,
but supple
now it feels worn and cracked and hurts for
moving and that's not even the end
it's just two weeks.
Pain don't always hurt full enough for moving
me, sometimes it hurts only for reminding
where I am that my own choices brought me
here and hold me down till all I do is move in
circles and sleep in the bed I made. But this
morning I needed a way for pulling myself back
into my skin and

feeling my insides move free of strings. So I got
up early, and while momma slept, I showered
hot and long
wiped the sweat from the bathroom mirror for
meeting my own eyes but it felt like a ghost, or
same as testing fate
i wouldn't even need no incantation, just staying
and staring long enough and then Candyman or
Bloody Mary'd be smiling a, 'what took you so
long', and I'm ashamed my first thought was
relief. What I managed was
padding soft and silent to my bedroom across
from momma's, I'd moved her from the room
shared with my stepdad for sanity, for walking in
and giving her night meds or carrying her to the
bathroom without feeling anger solid as hot
stones sliding down the back of me when I
listened to his snoring not even offering up
silence as a thing that could help.
I checked the crack I keep in her door when I
walked by looking for the rise and fall of her
chest and then came here for writing it down, for
making it plain, for fighting for something
keeping me from forgetting my own name
same as momma looking at me in the hospital
saying she'd like to see her Sam, all while I was
standing right there. So here's the promise or the
plan or the prayer, I'm going to fall in love. Not
a fairytale, but still such an impossibility

i might as well leave my window open for the
boohag to enter in. But I'm going to love, a him,
or her, or myself, or putting words on the page.
Something. Something's going to fit full in that
emotion again. Even with again meaning that
love space's been worn in, at least once, and I
love my mom, with my whole heart, even as
every day is screaming for break, for silence, to
not hear my name with a need attached to the
end, so that counts as love, and it doesn't, and it
does.

# Save Me

She said it was okay
that's why you're here with me
and I want to shake her and say
Sister, I am set out to sea
and he is the pull of the tide

# Choice

This body that I hate has grown
to recognize spite
it has fought back with
eyes wide open
it has crumbled apart
i am not this body
so full of seed and spit
and words broken over the
soft flesh of my thighs
i have watched from a distance
the way I trust his eyes
and this body believes
for the space of fuck
turned thick to hold
that eyes and hands
and lips mean love
as long as skin
can be made skin
and yes rings at the same
timber
as muffled moan
and for that I hate this body
i am too drowned to cry
this body soaked heavy
with sweat
the taste neither its

or mine
and silent
so silent when there are
words to be said
lyrical ones that
could pull down the moon
could rebuild Babylon
and rest tucked
safe
inside
i cannot be this
body
it is soft where it
shouldn't
curving so quick
fluid
it forgets primal
shape
silly as putty
till his hands
prove form
and tremble at
that
because left to
myself
i ain't fit to be seen
please set me free. From
this
body

# How to Live

I think about dying more than I should
i used to think about love, but it's
spelled different now
i think if momma had love
a man who didn't make her pray
over his promises
then it would be okay
and I could cry everyday
the seconds even, each of
them soaked through
it doesn't feel sad
most days coming
dying feels easier than hope
disappointment doesn't stop it
God already is
with me
besides I know how to preach it
words lined up to matter is easy
i shuffle, deal them out on the phone
in-person, and they look
- even on the phone I see
them - seeing the one I don't
sound like when I talk
the one who never wishes for
secrets soaked

the one brushing dirt off her shoulder
till a mountain lands behind me
and they say Strong like something to want
and I think the real me is there
dust-covered already
buried underneath

I thought about dying this morning
because it feels same as not liking
myself
and I have no time
for that
it's not just love though
same as any girl, at some point, not always
but sometimes
i thought it was spelled rescue
not so much safe
but soft
enough to lay in all the way
but love has been shovel-building
dust for mountains and I rise
up all willing to sink deeper
in the hole every time I believed
enough believing to build being alone
each of them looking at me
the same as love saying
i'm the one who got
away or should have been or should
be it echoes

same as thunder
or grief same as the sound of
anything the last being
the last
right at the second you know it's true
but it can't be same as love
now
now at 40 ain't love
i miss it, but my 40 knows missing is
the game, and I'm too poor to play

# Heritage

Southern lady
shade, "oh you still have
your maiden name" sounds
like a village cliff call
She Is Unwanted!
it is pain and pride
that mastery of shade locked
somewhere in my
DNA

# Promise to Keep

No more poems for them
no more
if it'll be heartbreak
it won't be them
not anymore
i will only crack
in new places
over ripe territory
but no more for them
not one more poem for them
past this one

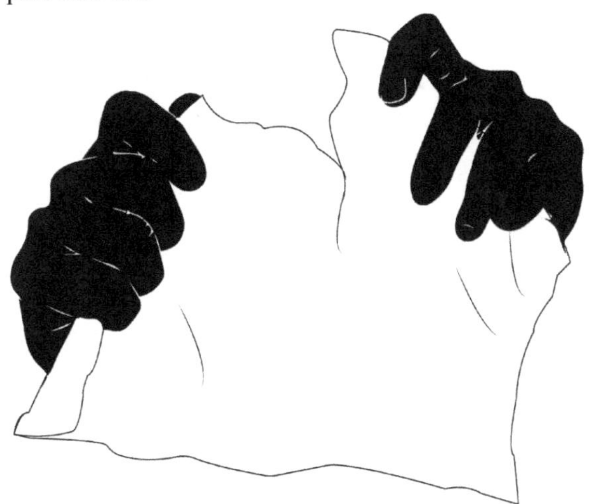

# Tuesday

Sad should have more words I
think should be a thing you
can hold so it sometimes makes
sense, it should speak back
and say just today or
forever so you know it
should say
built in or picked up so
it's clear if the ancestors
should be called or blamed

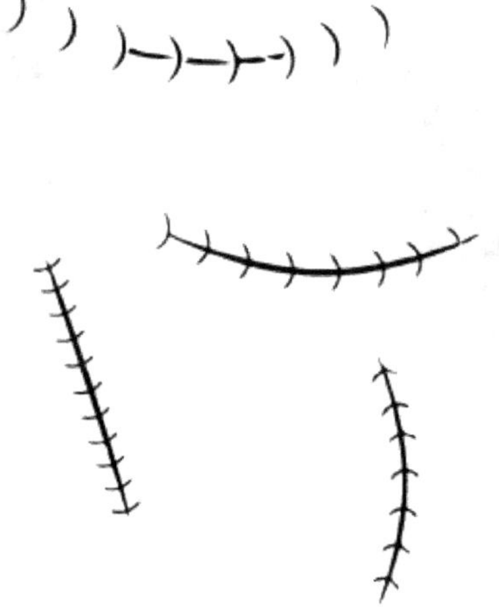

# Rehab 101

1. Stop thinking about him to bring him back -
necromancy is dangerous - let dead things lie
2. Stop drinking when it's easy feeling like
resurrection - refer to number 1

# Girl

i'm not the shout it from the rooftops
girl, not the, you're mine and
nobody else's girl, not the you're
crazy but I love you girl, have
been the we should have a threesome
girl, the what we drinking I
just happen to have condoms girl,
the I've always loved you but
let's keep it secret girl, the
you're everything I've ever wanted
should be my mistress girl - that
i've heard, never I waited for you
looked for you, held the air in
your shape til I found your fit girl
i am the even hold hands in
secret girl fingers stretching behind
or under to be felt but never seen
girl I am not the flesh made dreams
come true girl, I think of you
first in the morning girl but
yes to the always there girl,
it's been a minute but can I
come through girl, the what you mean
i don't think about you, I still
masturbate to you girl

you hold me down girl when
all I do is fly away looking
down at myself like
Girl.
Now I'm the, I don't even know
if I want it girl, the thought of love
makes me so tired girl, the
i think I done forgot what I
imagined girl, too smudged with bodies
and slick and sweet to see it
clear girl, the I should have known
better girl, by at least the third
time girl, the even with all that
i still hesitate when you ask girl
cause borrowed love sings better
than alone
Girl.

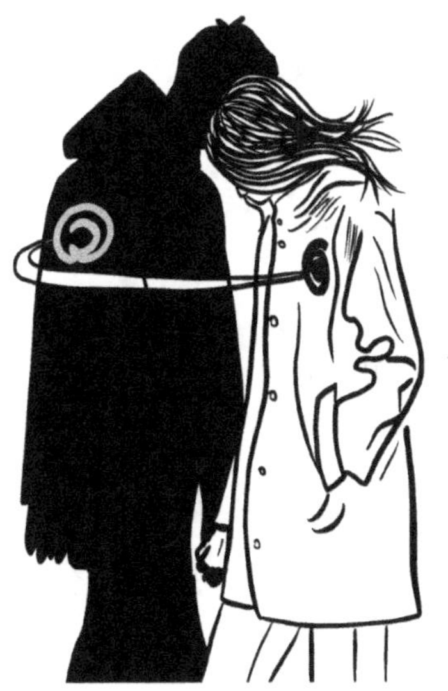

# Find Me Easy

I've been looking for rest
courting it, pleading
cause I can't hear past my heartbeat
or think unless it rains
and the excuse can be the reason
where are the soft spots
i need to line them up chained
together to hold fast
enough to cover the lie
cause those are good enough at being
found
i want to be gentle and kind
i want to smell like sunshine
to somebody enough to
pull close and pocket
enough to be saved and I can
hunker down there in darkness
held together made
whole or at most just
barely broken smooth
dust free beautiful a
brown that shines
shimmers
smooths
welcomes and alone

is as lost as rest used
to be a dream I can't remember
a song I forget to sing a thing
crushed in my fingers and blown
same as wishes or the heavy
of regret sent in search
of new anchors

# Sunshine & Rain

Today was a good day
in dreams these things happen
looking at you thinking
how close to perfect and
how much I don't care why
or about good or right or
holy or sane even, not
when days feel like today
i don't care who you go back to
what life you're leaving when
not giving shade to mine
i'll hold onto the foolish with both hands
i'll stare it in it's face promising never
letting go because
today was good
as something blurred at the edges
and soft for leaning
it was smiles I couldn't stop
even with the shadow of tomorrow
keeping pace with your shoulder
i don't care, about as much
as I should care, let me live and die
in today, I'd die a borrowed death
and it'd still be worth the rise and fall of
every last exhale coated thick heavy

shining with bold sun brightness it blinds
good and well

# Laundry Day

a soul will find itself
i think its hands are steady open I
think it lacks sleep or tears but
is good at sharing well enough
it only lays claim to purpose and
doesn't question why
it is impatient with
the end sees time same as smoke
in the mouth how
close to happy leaning into
the waiting must be how full
and round a soul must be what
else has power to pull the moon
change the tide lift the sky
close enough for touching or believing
or letting go I would trade a
life for a soul this life
even an offering wrung dry
hung in the sun see-through
in the burned places
eager to be worn in moonlight
rubbed raw by lapping tide
with new and skin flexible
for a soul to hold

# Reincarnation

the problem is the skeleton built
i been placing those bones
swiping them clean polishing
to shine since I was old enough for
counting old enough for needing
the angle and bend to be just so

right enough I could shut my eyes
climb inside feel the warm of
flesh steady beating sounding
low and secret-like held in my throat
i been building them bones into

something I been needing close
or not they fall every time
i cry over the ash like it's new
same as if it won't coming even
past being old enough to count

with hands wrinkled soft
with bones death-rattling dry

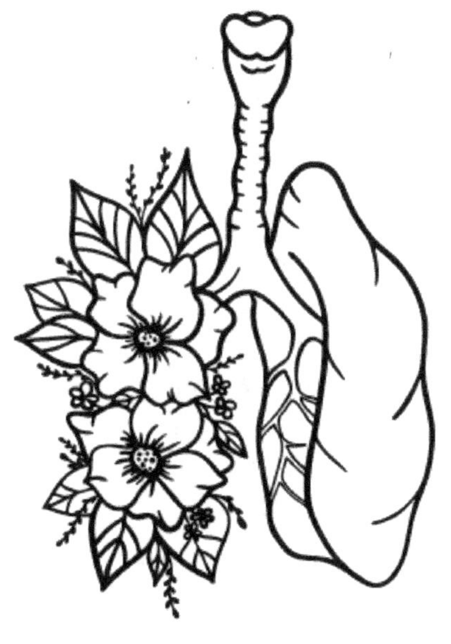

# Try Harder

You can pull love from the sky
that's what they say like it lives
in sunsets like it's waiting to be
labeled easy like I ain't been
trying at being easy
slight and light
asking for
nothing save for warmth maybe
or forever or the end of
guessing or wondering or throwing
hope over my shoulder trailing behind
a shadow refusing to offer any shade
i see blue in the sky clouds a
fake soft rainbows see-thru
sunsets bold enough for stopping
to see but love don't live
there at least not
for me

# Tears of a Clown

oh my you have made a fool of me
the air is soft and I ain't afraid of falling
through I can breathe and my brain dims
to subtle and kind I digest different
bits of you every time silent when I
chew greedy when I swallow
i like the way you smell the
comfort heat of you in sheets I remember
you on purpose I practice saying
your name and snatch the echo close

# Please

Tell me you love me
Say it again and again
Reach it in your fingertips
Cause it's too late for me
My skin is open

# Say Yes

that love built in waiting
the one saying years are silent
footsteps hope ground down
like gold dust hidden in pockets
coating fingers the one whispering
soon come soon be
rubbed over mistakes and
decisions fear threw on your back
till you said thank you and carried
the one claiming rest
stop see breathe the one
pouring settle sweet as lavender
into your heels steady as a
rocking chair bathed in southern
sunset the round welcome of sweet tea
coating the tongue
the one feeling like skin of your
skin bone of your bone
home of your home
that love calms like ocean
that love remembers your name

www.ingramcontent.com/pod-product-compliance
Lightning Source LLC
LaVergne TN
LVHW050943200726
843508LV00011B/2425